THE COMPLETE
WHY DO WE
SAY THAT?
CARTOONS BY *Larry*

Compiled by
Graham Donaldson & Maris Ross

DAVID & CHARLES
Newton Abbot   London

A CIP catalogue record for this book is
available from the British Library

Copyright © Graham Donaldson and
Maris Ross 1990

First published 1990
Reprinted 1991

The right of Graham Donaldson and
Maris Ross to be identified as authors of
this work has been asserted by them in
accordance with the Copyright, Designs
and Patents Act 1988.

Printed in Great Britain
by Billings & Sons Ltd, Worcester
for David & Charles plc
Brunel House   Newton Abbot   Devon

Introduction

When we use expressions like 'He's leading the life of Reilly' or 'That's a load of old codswallop' we take it for granted that people automatically know what we mean – usually, they do.

But how many people know the origins of these everyday sayings, many of which go back centuries?

In some cases the roots are irretrievably lost in the mists of antiquity. In other cases, more than one theory exists for an expression's origin. And in still other cases, confusion has arisen when an existing saying has been adopted to fit a new circumstance.

For example, the saying 'Nine-day wonder' which originally referred to the time-span normally taken by new-born kittens or puppies to open their eyes, subsequently neatly fitted the unfortunate fate of Lady Jane Grey who reigned as Queen of England for nine days in July, 1553, before being executed the following year. Her plight is often – we believe incorrectly – put forward as the basis of the 'Nine-day wonder' expression.

The origins of many everyday sayings listed in this book *are* beyond dispute. Where differing theories do exist we have selected the one we consider to be the most likely.

The delights and surprises contained in these pages will undoubtedly leave you feeling 'over the moon'. Talking of which . . .

Buying a pig in a poke

At some time or other we've all been warned not to buy a 'pig in a poke'! But how did that saying originally come about?

To buy a pig in a poke means that you have been cheated. Back in Saxon times a suckling pig would be taken to market and sold in a sack, or poke. However, there were some shady characters around, and an unsuspecting buyer could find that a cat had been substituted for a pig in the poke.

STEAL HIS THUNDER

Stealing someone's thunder means to take glory or attention away from him. John Dennis, a seventeenth-century English dramatist, was the first man literally to have his thunder stolen.

For his play *Appius and Virginia*, he invented a new sound effects device to reproduce thunder, filling the auditorium with a loud rumble from a gadget that looked like a wooden trough. But audiences did not like the play and the management of the Drury Lane Theatre brought the curtain down after a very short run and staged Shakespeare's *Macbeth* instead.

When a roll of thunder sounded at the appropriate scene in *Macbeth*, Dennis complained, 'That is my thunder, by God! The villains will play my thunder, but not my plays.'

Alas for him, he wrote more unsuccessful plays than successful ones but was better remembered as a critic.

A feather in your cap

If your boss said this to you it would mean that you had done something praiseworthy and had gone up in his estimation. It goes back to the days when the Red Indians were on the warpath. For every enemy a brave killed he was allowed to add a feather to his head-dress.

TURN A BLIND EYE

Viscount Horatio Nelson, Britain's most famous naval hero, was responsible for 'turning a blind eye', meaning that he ignored an event.

At the naval battle of Copenhagen in 1801, Nelson was subordinate to Sir Hyde Parker, who hoisted the flag signalling the British ships to withdraw as he felt Danish resistance was stronger than expected.

'Now damn me if I do,' Nelson said. 'I have a right to be blind sometimes.' He put his spyglass to his right eye, whose sight he had lost from shell fragments seven years earlier. Then he added, 'I really do not see the signal.'

He carried on the fight instead of retreating, and the Danish ships ended up surrendering.

Crocodile tears

To weep crocodile tears means to fake sadness. If you were to look closely (but not too closely!) at a crocodile while he was eating a large meal you would see tears in his eyes. You could be excused for thinking he was a bit upset for his victim. Not a bit of it.

In fact the crocodile has a duct at the corner of each eye which automatically releases 'tears' when he opens his jaws wide. He may look sorry for his victim but don't you believe it. He's just shedding 'crocodile tears'.

LAUGH UP YOUR SLEEVE

If you have secret grounds for amusement, you laugh up your sleeve. This was exactly what people used to do centuries ago.

In the Middle Ages, sleeves were very wide. If you wanted to enjoy a private joke, you could raise your arm and use the sleeve to screen your face. By the sixteenth century, sleeves became narrower but people still spoke of laughing up their sleeve.

The boot's on the other foot

Today, this expression is used when a situation is quite the reverse of what it was originally. It was only 200 years ago that footwear makers began manufacturing left and right shoes and boots. Before that, they were the same for both feet.

A man who tried on his new boots often found that if one of them hurt, his problem could be solved by swapping them over. A total change had come about – the boot was on the other foot.

ON TENTERHOOKS

A good book or drama will keep you on tenterhooks, in a state of tension or suspense about the outcome.

The phrase comes from the days before textile mills, when cloth was stretched on wooden frames called tenters. Bent nails were set around the frame as the hooks on which to stretch the fabric. These tenter hooks got their name from the Latin verb to stretch, *tendere*, and were useful for hanging other objects, like carcasses of meat.

A pretty kettle of fish

When somebody lands in a tricky, difficult, or awkward situation, they might well say, 'this is a pretty kettle of fish'.

Years ago it was the custom in the Border regions of Scotland to go on riverside picnics where salmon would be caught, boiled on the riverside in a kettle – a cooking pan – and eaten on the spot. Such picnics became known as a 'kettle of fish'.

The word 'pretty' originally meant 'tricky'. So, when the picnickers were having trouble landing their salmon, which apparently happened a lot, they would be faced with a pretty kettle of fish.

HOIST WITH HIS OWN PETARD

A person hoist with his own petard has become the victim of his own scheme. He sets out to injure someone else but the plan backfires and traps him instead.

A petard was a siege weapon in the sixteenth and seventeenth centuries. Gun powder was put in a metal or wooden box and used to blow a hole in the weak point of fortifications. But the contraption was so erratic that whoever lit the fuse risked blowing themselves up.

Shakespeare was alive when the petard was in use. In *Hamlet*, he portrays Polonius, who wants to trap Hamlet, as hoist with his own petard.

Back to square one

This means that a plan has been abandoned and you are starting again from the beginning. It comes from the early days of radio commentaries on football matches before the likes of Brian Moore or John Motson.

To make it easier for the listener to follow the game, a diagram of the pitch was published, divided into squares and the commentator would continually refer to which square the ball was in.

The goalkeeper was in square one and if the ball was returned to him by a defender to start a fresh attack, it was 'back to square one'.

SLEEP LIKE A TOP

The wooden spinning top is one of the oldest of toys, an unlikely source of comparison with anyone who enjoys a deep sleep.

But the people of medieval times were fascinated by the toy. They noticed that when it spun round fast enough, perfectly balanced on its point, the top appeared not to move. They joked that the top was asleep. As far back as 1616, sound sleepers were therefore described as 'sleeping like a top'.

Climb on the bandwagon

This saying is used to describe anybody who joins in with something that looks like it will be a success, so that they can make a profit for themselves.

It comes from the days when a band used to play on a wagon driven through the streets of towns in the southern States of America to advertise religious or political meetings.

When there was an election, important people would climb on the bandwagon to demonstrate their support for a candidate.

To BLACKBALL SOMEONE

When someone is blackballed, they are ostracised by society. The term harks back to the heyday of gentlemen's clubs in the eighteenth and nineteenth centuries.

Entry into venerable institutions like the Athenaeum in London depended on the vote of one's fellows as to eligibility. The ballot was an anonymous one. If the existing members agreed with the suitability of an applicant, they put a white wooden or ivory ball in the voting box. If they wanted to shun the applicant, they signified their negative vote with a black ball.

To strike while the iron is hot

If you act at exactly the right time, then you strike while the iron is hot and things work out just right. It is a saying that goes back hundreds of years and refers, not surprisingly, to the skills of the village blacksmith.

His experience and knowledge enabled him to know just when to start hammering on a horseshoe to form the right shape. It would work only when the metal was just at the right temperature. He had to strike while the iron was hot.

TO STONEWALL

The stonewaller is well known in politics, business and cricket. He stands unmoved, resolute in his defensive efforts to thwart the proceedings.

The name goes back to a Confederate general in the American civil war, Thomas Jonathan Jackson, and his defence at the Battle of Bull Run in 1861. Someone in the heat of the fight was heard to shout, 'Look, there's Jackson standing like a stone wall.' His troops promptly became known as the Stonewall Brigade and the nickname stuck with the general.

A sad footnote: Stonewall Jackson was accidentally shot and killed by his own side in another battle two years later.

Eating humble pie

To eat humble pie means to be humiliated, to admit others know best or are superior in some way.

The saying comes from the days when the Lord of the Manor and his fellow huntsmen feasted on the spoils of their day's hunting. They ate prime venison, while the servants and others of low standing had to make do with a pie made from the umbles of the deer – its entrails, liver and heart.

PYRRHIC VICTORY

At times victory can be a costly affair, with the winner no better off than the loser. The First World War contained many examples of Pyrrhic victories when long, bloody battles achieved little while thousands died on both sides.

King Pyrrhus, a land-hungry warrior who ruled part of Greece from the age of twelve, would have been at home on these battlefields. In the third century BC he set out to conquer Italy. After winning the Battle of Asculum in 279 BC by sacrificing some of his best troops, he is supposed to have said, 'One more such victory and we are lost.' So, a Pyrrhic victory is one where the cost is too high.

Bring home the bacon

To 'bring home the bacon' is to return home triumphantly, having achieved some plan or objective, perhaps a pay rise or promotion at work.

The saying refers to the custom of the Dunmow Flitch which dates back nearly 900 years. Any person kneeling at the church door in the village of Dunmow, Essex, who swore that for a year and a day he had never had an argument with his wife or wished himself unmarried, could claim an award. It was a flitch (or side) of bacon. But only eight people won it in more than 500 years.

HOBSON'S CHOICE

When you have no choice at all, this is known as Hobson's choice. Back in the seventeenth century, Hobson was a carrier of goods and packages in the English university town of Cambridge. He also hired out horses. But customers were never allowed to pick and choose.

If they wanted one of Mr Hobson's horses, they had to take the one standing nearest the stable door or none at all. So they had Hobson's choice – or nothing.

Despite this idiosyncrasy, Hobson was a valued citizen. He helped to provide Cambridge with a badly needed clean water supply in 1606. To this day he is still remembered with a street, a fountain and a stream named after him.

I could sleep on a clothes line

When people are really exhausted and tired out, they sometimes say 'I could sleep on a clothes line'.

They are lucky they don't have to. In the last century in big cities like London, poor people had to do just that.

Landlords of inns used to charge people twopence a night to sleep sitting up on a bench, leaning against a line stretched tight in front of them. It was known as the 'twopenny rope'. Often, callous landlords would wake their guests in the morning simply by cutting the rope.

TEDDY BEAR

The teddy bear is the favourite toy of millions of children. When they grow up, Teddy is still remembered with affection and even passed on to children's children. But how did he get his name?

Oddly enough, an American president is responsible. Theodore Roosevelt, whose nickname was Teddy, was invited on a hunting trip in Mississippi in 1903. His host, wishing to ensure that the President bagged something, caught and stunned a small bear and left it at a pre-arranged spot. Roosevelt, however, discovered the trick and would have nothing to do with it.

When the story emerged, the *Washington Post* published a cartoon of the scene. This was too good an opportunity for toy manufacturers to miss. They immediately renamed their line in cuddly stuffed bears as teddy bears.

A nine-day wonder

Something that is very popular for a while and then loses its appeal is said to be 'a nine-day wonder'.

The saying is said to come from the plight of newborn puppies and kittens which are, of course, blind at birth. Generally, their eyes open about the ninth day of their lives.

So for the first nine days all is wondrous and mysterious. After that they can see things clearly and the world around them becomes commonplace and taken for granted. The 'nine-day wonder' is past.

CAN'T HOLD A CANDLE TO HIM

Soccer fans discussing their heroes might well say, 'Smith? He can't hold a candle to Jones.' This means the talent of Smith is nowhere near that of Jones.

The saying goes back to the seventeenth century when link-boys carried torches to show travellers along London's streets after dark. They hired themselves out by crying, 'Have a light, gentlemen?' The task did not require much intelligence and was a very subordinate position. So, if you wanted to insult someone, you would say, 'He's not fit to hold a candle to anyone.'

Nineteen to the dozen

This saying is used of somebody who talks very quickly. Patrick Moore, who presents the TV programme, The Sky at Night, is often said to be talking 'nineteen to the dozen'.

The expression came about in the tin and copper mines of Cornwall which were often hit by disastrous floods. But in the eighteenth-century, steam-powered pumping engines were invented to clear the water. At the peak of their efficiency the pumps were said to be working at 'nineteen to the dozen', meaning that they were pumping out 19,000 gallons of water for every twelve bushels of coal needed to keep the engines going.

GET OUT OF BED
ON THE WRONG SIDE

You know the feeling when everything seems wrong. You are moody and cross. Someone is bound to tell you that you got out of bed on the wrong side.

The wrong side is the left, associated with bad luck in old superstitions because the devil lived on the left side of God before being banished. The right side is therefore considered the lucky side, so if you 'put your best foot forward,' it is the right foot. That is the side to favour, if you want the spirits to smile on you.

Having an axe to grind

This saying describes a person who tries to persuade somebody else to adopt a course of action without revealing their own selfish interest.

The saying comes from a story told by American inventor Benjamin Franklin. When he was young, a man brought an axe into the yard where Franklin was working and asked the boy to show him how the grindstone worked. When, after much hard work, the axe was ground, the man laughed at Franklin and left, carrying his newly sharpened axe.

THE REAL McCOY

'Now *that* is the real McCoy', a connoisseur might say when he comes across the genuine article.

The saying could have originated in Scotland around 1870 when a whisky distiller called G. Mackay promoted his whisky as 'the real Mackay' to distinguish it from a rival company also called Mackay.

Then 'Kid' McCoy, an American prize fighter in the 1890s, liked to boast that someone in a bar challenged him to prove his identity. So McCoy knocked the unfortunate person out and when he came round, he agreed, 'You're the real McCoy!'

Equally colourful is the story of Bill McCoy, who smuggled whisky from Canada into the United States during the prohibition era. He was proud to claim his whisky was 'the real McCoy', not home distilled.

Possession is nine points of the law

Somebody who uses this saying is claiming to have an overwhelming advantage over his opponent in a quarrel. He is saying that his case is so strong it would be very difficult for the other person to win.

The original nine points of the law were; 1 A lot of money; 2 A lot of patience; 3 A good cause; 4 A good lawyer; 5 A good counsel; 6 Good witnesses; 7 A good jury; 8 A good judge; 9 Good luck!

THE DEVIL TO PAY

In the days of wooden ships, the devil was the name for the longest seam of the hull. Every so often it had to be caulked or 'paid', an awkward job as the vessel had to be tipped on its side between tides.

The seam was then sealed with hot pitch. Serious trouble loomed, as the phrase now means, when sailors had 'the devil to pay and no pitch hot', to use the full phrase.

Bury the hatchet

People who have been locked in an argument for some time might well decide at some stage to 'bury the hatchet'. In other words, they will end their feud and forget their differences.

When one of the North American Indian tribes wanted to end a war, either against another tribe or against the white man, the first thing was to smoke the peace-pipe. Then they would be 'commanded by the Great Spirit' to bury their hatchets, knives and other weapons as a positive sign of their wish for peace.

GORDON BENNETT

Who was he, this man whose name we use when we are told something remarkable, extraordinary, amazing? Well, he was remarkable, extraordinary and amazing.

For instance, he was the man who despatched Henry Stanley to deepest Africa in 1871 to find Dr Livingstone, no expense spared. As editor of the *New York Herald*, he was such a lavish spender that he was reputed to have spent thirty million dollars of the newspaper's revenue on such ventures. Another of his amazing scoops was the news that General Custer and his men had been massacred by Indians.

He established the Paris edition of the *New York Herald* in 1887. His high spending continued there. When he could not get a table in a busy restaurant, he bought the place so that he could sit down to mutton chops. Then he told a waiter that he could keep the restaurant on condition that chips were always on the menu and that a table was always available for Gordon Bennett. What more can one say than . . . Gordon Bennett!

Lock, stock and barrel

If somebody emigrated to Australia they might decide to sell their house and contents – 'lock, stock and barrel'. In other words, everything they possess. The phrase means something in its entirety.

Its origins, however, have nothing to do with door locks, shop stocks or barrels of beer. It is simply an old military reference to mean everything, the whole lot . . . the lock, stock and barrel of a firearm is the complete gun.

IN THE DOGHOUSE

You have got to be a bit of a saint not to have spent some time in the doghouse. It means that you are in disgrace.

The first person to be sent 'to the doghouse' was Mr Darling in *Peter Pan*, the ever popular children's play written by Sir James Matthew Barrie in 1904. Mr Darling, the children's father, is beastly to Nana, their dog, and chains it up outside. As his punishment, he lives in the doghouse until the children come home from their adventures.

At sixes and sevens

A person is said to be 'all at sixes and sevens' when he is faced with a difficult problem and just doesn't know what to do.

The phrase comes from a dispute in the middle ages between two of the craftsmen's guilds in the City of London. The Merchant Taylors and the Skinners were both founded within a few days of each other in 1327, five other guilds having already been chartered. For nearly fifty years they argued about which was to go sixth and seventh in processions. Finally, in 1484, the Lord Mayor ruled that they should take it in turns — whoever was sixth one year, would be seventh the next . . . and so on.

HIT A SNAG

Life seldom runs smoothly. Suddenly a problem rears its head. Things have hit a snag.

Why a snag? This word is Scandinavian in origin and meant spike or jagged projection. Migrants took the word to America where it was a common comment on the river boats when they hit a tree stump hidden in the water.

Gradually the word took on a wider meaning. In 1886, the London *Pall Mall Gazette* said, 'Our extradition treaty with the United States has run up against its first snag, to use an expression familiar on the Mississippi.'

The Best Man

He, of course, is the chap who remembers the ring, reads the telegrams, and generally helps the bridegroom at a wedding.

According to Scottish legend, however, his duties used to be much more demanding. For it was customary for a man in love simply to kidnap and unceremoniously carry off the woman he had fallen for. He would choose good friends to help him in the task – groomsmen – and the bravest became known as the 'Best Man'.

The bride's closest friends – bridesmaids – were supposed to help her defend herself against her abductors. No doubt they both lived happily ever after!

A COCK-AND-BULL STORY

In the heyday of travel by coach and horses, the Cock and the Bull were two flourishing English inns that stood side by side on the main road fifty miles north of London.

The London-bound coaches pulled into one inn and the outward-bound coaches stopped at the other to change teams of horses and, naturally enough, bring news from their towns of origin. The gossip grew more exaggerated in bouncing back and forth between inn customers.

The tales were so outlandish that any incredible or misleading yarn was labelled a cock-and-bull story. The inn buildings still exist in Stony Stratford, now part of the new city of Milton Keynes, but the coaches stopped calling when the railways were built in the nineteenth century.

A whipping boy

A person who is punished or blamed for an offence that somebody else has committed is often known as 'a whipping boy'.

In the middle ages it was common practice in European countries for a boy of common birth to be educated alongside a royal prince. But he paid heavily for the privilege. If the prince did something wrong, discipline demanded that punishment be inflicted. But there was no question of the royal bottom being spanked; the commoner had to step (or rather, bend) forward and he was flogged instead. Such was life for a 'whipping boy'.

FALL GUY

The fall guy takes the blame. His rough time began in the 1920s when rigged wrestling matches became common in the United States.

He would agree to participate in a match and take a prearranged 'fall' to make the prize wrestler look good. The phrase took on the connotation of being deceived into taking the rap, because the fall guy was often badly beaten up instead of getting the promised light treatment from his victorious opponent.

Get your goat

If somebody 'gets your goat', they annoy, irritate, or generally make you angry. And if, years ago, you were a racehourse owner, you would have had good reason to be upset for it was a trick of the trade to stable a thoroughbred racehorse with a goat, the belief being that the presence of the smaller animal kept the horse calm and composed. Knowing this, it was not uncommon for some rascals to break in, separate the two animals, thus upsetting the highly-strung horse and probably causing it to lose the following day's race.

This deed would certainly 'get the goat' of the horse's owner.

THAT'S MY BUGBEAR

What a bugbear! You might well say that when a problem causes anxiety or dread.

Bwg, pronounced bug, is the Welsh word for ghost or hobgoblin. Of course, a bear is a pretty frightening creature. Join the two together as they did in the sixteenth century, and a make-believe monster is created to carry children away if they are naughty. Down the years, the disciplinarians of the nursery also used bogeymen, bogles and bug-a-boos, all mischievous spirits from the same origin, to frighten children into good behaviour.

Dressed to the nines

This saying simply means that you have put on your very smartest clothes, probably because you are off to an important function like a wedding, a formal dinner, or perhaps a job interview.

It is a very old expression and, although its origins are uncertain, it is believed to have started off as dressed 'to the eyes'. That meant, of course, smartly dressed from head to foot.

In medieval English the saying would have been 'dressed to then eyne'. Over the centuries it is thought to have gradually changed into 'to the nines'.

HAMMER AND TONGS

A couple going for each other 'hammer and tongs' are quarreling with all the energy at their command. The phrase harks back to the days when a blacksmith made all sorts of metal objects in addition to horse shoes.

He took the hot metal straight from the forge, holding it steady with tongs in one hand while beating it into shape with a hammer in the other. He always had to work as quickly as possible before the iron cooled and was no longer malleable. Anyone who pursues a target with all the force at their command therefore came to be known as going at it hammer and tongs.

Soccer hooligans

Soccer hooligans have alas, figured all too often in the news in recent times.

The word hooliganism became established at the end of the nineteenth century when an Irish family named Hooligan lived in Southwark, south-east London. By all accounts they were such a rowdy, noisy and badly-behaved bunch that their reputation as trouble-makers spread far and wide.

Ever since, any group of youths who cause problems with their anti-social behaviour have been called 'hooligans'.

CHEW THE FAT

To chew the fat means to talk a long time, usually in a grumbling way over some grievance, which is exactly what sailors used to do about the food aboard ship.

The old way of preserving meat was to pack it in barrels of brine, and salt beef was one of the few staples that could last through a long voyage. But the salt curing process made the beef very tough. The seamen had to chew endlessly to swallow the unpalatable and fatty meat down. At least it gave them an off duty chance to chat, usually grumbling that 'God made the vittles but the devil made the cook.'

Ye olde tea shoppe

Places such as the famous Ye Olde Cheshire Cheese Inn in Fleet Street and Ye Olde Tea Shoppes throughout the country are said to be steeped in antiquity. So they may be. But their names are also steeped in error.

In the ancient alphabet used until the end of the middle ages the letters 'th' were represented by a single character which looked like our present 'y'. So when the word 'the' was transcribed from the old texts it was written down as 'ye'. It was never in fact pronounced as 'yee' and so to do so is nonsense. For what we have is the simple mis-spelling of the everyday word 'the'.

That has led to fanciful elaborations like Ye Olde Tea Shoppe. Ah well, don't tell ye touristes!

LICK INTO SHAPE

Unlikely as it sounds in today's state of knowledge, our ancestors believed certain animals were born formless and their mothers licked them into shape.

This false notion especially applied in the fifteenth century to bears, fiercely protective creatures which did not allow humans near their young. All the distant observer could see was the large bear licking a bundle of fur.

In fact she was cleaning her cub. Appropriately the saying 'lick into shape' now means making something presentable or moulding it into a system.

Worth his salt

Anybody 'worth his salt' is doing a good job, whether it's at work, as part of a team or in any situation where others rely on his efforts.

In Roman times, salt was considered vital for health and well-being, but often difficult to come by. So soldiers were actually paid partly in money and partly in salt. Later they were given an allowance so that they could buy their salt themselves and this money was known by the Latin name 'salarium' – meaning 'of salt'.

That's where our word salary – payment for work done – comes from.

IN QUARANTINE

Quarantine means exclusion from the company of others and comes from the Latin word for forty.

Quarantine was especially applied to sailing ships when it was realized that travellers spread contagious diseases. The original number of days of isolation imposed on a ship was forty before those aboard could enter port and mix with the inhabitants.

For English noblewomen in the seventeenth and eighteenth centuries, quarantine held another meaning. When their husbands died, some widows had to remove from the main mansion of the estate to a smaller 'dower' house while the larger home passed to the heir of the next generation. But for forty days, known as the widow's quarantine, a woman could remain in her late husband's mansion.

Nest egg

Thrifty people who have regularly put away money in savings are often said to have built up 'a nice nest egg'. At one time, poultry farmers used to put a fake egg – usually made of porcelain – in a hen's nest, believing the bird would then be encouraged to lay more eggs. In the same way, a 'nest egg' came to refer to a person's savings.

USING YOUR LOAF

The Cockneys, or East Enders of London, are famous for their rhyming slang. Using your loaf, meaning to use your common sense, rhymes loaf of bread with head.

But it also rhymes with dead, and the first use of the phrase was in the trenches of World War I when 'Duck your loaf' was the terse Cockney instruction to keep your head below the trench or end up dead. Between the wars, Cockney sergeants started saying 'use your loaf' to chivvy recruits who were slow at following orders.

Black sheep of the family

In a large family there is bound to be a boy or girl who never seems to do well or is always in trouble. He or she is 'the black sheep of the family'.

For years, shepherds believed that black sheep were a problem: their coat was valueless and it was believed (wrongly) that their colour frightened other sheep. The expression gradually came to apply to troublesome humans.

THROW IN THE SPONGE

In the prize fights of the nineteenth century, the sponge used to wipe
the contestants' faces would be thrown in the air, signalling that it
would not be needed any more, when one of the contestants wanted
to surrender.

Nowadays we talk of throwing in the sponge to mean giving up or
surrendering. In boxing, a towel is still thrown into the ring by the
second to signal that the fighter is giving up.

Beating about the bush

Somebody who beats about the bush has the annoying habit of not saying exactly what they mean, but talking round the point.

It's a very old saying which comes from hunting. Specially hired people – known as 'beaters' literally beat bushes and startled game birds into the air. As soon as the waiting hunter saw his target in flight, he would immediately open fire. Unlike his colleague, he was a man of direct action and would certainly not be 'beating about the bush'.

PIPE DOWN

Orders are still piped in the navy, harking back to when they were whistled by the boatswain. The last pipe of the day on a warship is called the pipe down.

This signals the order for silence and lights to be dimmed so that sailors not keeping the night watch can sleep. The phrase came ashore as a way to ask people to stop making a noise.

Merry Christmas

Wishing each other 'Merry Christmas' by sending a greetings card is a fairly new idea and one which had a troublesome beginning.

The first Christmas card to go on sale appeared in 1846. The picture on the front showed a family clearly in festive mood, happily drinking wine. And that's what caused the trouble. Church leaders and temperance organisations protested that the card depicted Christmas merely as a time for drinking and jollity. Nevertheless, sales went well.

In the 1870s a firm of art printers called Tucks began producing Christmas cards. The idea then really took off and developed into the multi-million pound business it is today.

QUIZ

Mr Daly, the manager of a Dublin theatre in the 1780s, laid a bet that he could introduce a new and meaningless word into the English language within twenty-four hours.

He chalked the word QUIZ on various walls within public view and, sure enough, within twenty-four hours Dubliners were inquiring what quiz meant. Mr Daly may also have known some Latin because *quis* means 'who' or 'what' in Latin.

After his escapade, it came to mean questioning, though in his era it also signified a practical joke or eccentric person. Little did he know the quiz games that were to follow on radio and television.

New Scotland Yard

Scotland Yard is probably the most famous police headquarters in the world and the focus of countless films and books by thriller writers.

Detective work reveals that the centre got its name from the street where it was originally located, Great Scotland Yard, Whitehall. That name came from the site of a castle used 1,000 years ago by the kings of Scotland who had to travel down and stay there once a year to pay allegiance to the English court.

In 1967, New Scotland Yard was established in Broadway, Westminster.

GONE TO POT

A person or institution gone to pot has been neglected beyond the point of salvation. The saying alludes to the days when broken items of gold and silver were thrown back into the melting pot if considered beyond repair.

The metal from stolen jewellery met the same fate, so that it could not be identified.

Gone to the dogs had the same meaning of ruin from the sixteenth century, when the leftovers that nobody else wanted were thrown to the dogs. Then as now, it was also abusive to compare a man with a dog.

Keep danger at bay

When people try to prevent the onset of a disaster, an illness, or some other unfortunate event, they are said to be 'keeping it at bay'. Over the centuries the bay laurel tree has been regarded by man as one of his great protectors. The Greeks and Romans, noting that the tree never seemed to be struck by lightning, used to wear its leaves on their heads as protection during thunderstorms.

Much later, during the Great Plague of London in 1665, people in their desperation turned to laurel leaves to protect them against the deadly affliction. They believed (wrongly – as 80,000 victims proved), that the leaves would keep the plague 'at bay'.

SWAN SONG

The ancient Greeks believed that the soul of Apollo, their god of music, passed into a swan and that because of this every swan sang beautifully just before it died.

Although the idea was false, great names of literature such as Chaucer, Shakespeare and Tennyson took up the theme. Swan song came to mean the last work of a composer, poet or actor before his death or retirement.

A baron of beef

A baron of beef is a magnificent double slice of meat not separated at the backbone. A single slice is called a sirloin. It is said that Henry VIII was so enraptured by one mouth-watering hunk that he 'knighted' it – thus sir-loin. Nice story, but nonsense. The word is older than Henry VIII and comes from the French sur (over) and longe (loin).

But it is thought that some eighteenth-century English aristocrats named a double sirloin a 'baron' because a baron is a step up from a knight.

GET DOWN TO BRASS TACKS

Choosing the right fabric was a lengthy business of looking at rolls in the old-fashioned draper's shop. When you had finally decided which one you wanted, you got down to brass tacks.

The brass tacks or nails were hammered at one yard intervals along the counter and the shopkeeper measured out how many yards of material you wanted. The nails were later replaced by measuring rules, but getting down to brass tacks still means to be practical or to get down to basics.

A scapegoat

Somebody who is made to take the blame for the actions of another person is said to be a 'scapegoat'.

In the Old Testament, a goat is chosen to bear the sins of the people. It is led into the wilderness and abandoned, taking their sins with it.

Scape is believed to be a shortened form of escape. So in the Old Testament story the people 'escape' the responsibility of their sins by loading them on to the goat.

RED LETTER DAY

Five centuries ago, ecclesiastical calendars started using red pigment on parchment to denote saints' days and church festivals among the black lettering of other days.

They came to be associated with memorable events, often signifying a day off and celebration at a fair. A red letter day is still synonymous with a happy special occasion.

Pop goes the weasel

Most of us remember the words of the nursery rhyme: 'Up and down the City Road; In and out the Eagle; That's the way the money goes; Pop goes the Weasel!'

Like most nursery rhymes, there is a story behind these seemingly meaningless words. The Eagle was the name of a pub in the City Road in London and it was a popular meeting place for people who worked in the hatmaking trade nearby. When short of funds some of them would 'pop' – that is, pawn – their weasel, or tool of their trade, to raise money for more drinks. Shame on them . . .

MOONLIGHTING

By the light of the moon, various people used to engage on illicit acts. In Ireland, gangs of men acting for landlords were called moonlighters when they attacked tenants to try to force them out.

Much more recently, moonlighting has come to mean doing a second paid job, usually at night, on top of holding down a steady job by day.

He's a toady!

This saying is used to criticise somebody who, to further his own ends, says or does anything to please his superior.

It comes from the days of travelling medicine men in the American 'Wild West'. They used to sell usually useless potions to the public. Taking advantage of the popular but false belief that toads were extremely poisonous, the 'quack' doctor would get an accomplice to swallow, or pretend to swallow, a toad. He would then immediately drink one of the doctor's portions and, much to the amazement of the crowd, walk away fit and well.

FORLORN HOPE

The *verloren hoop*, being the Dutch for lost troop, were the body of men picked to lead a storming party, knowing their lives would probably be lost in the attack.

The first use of forlorn hope in the English language in the sixteenth century also described them as the troop going first into battle and falling to make a passage for the rest. Forlorn hope came to indicate any perilous or desperate enterprise.

Scot-free

Scot, or sceot as it used to be spelt, was a form of taxation levied in olden times. Sometimes very poor people were excused payment. They were allowed to be sceot-free. Today the expression applies to anybody who gets out of a difficult situation unharmed.

GO FROM PILLAR TO POST

This is a very old phrase, and when first used in the fifteenth century it was the other way round: going from post to pillar.

Its origin lies in the first games of tennis, which began in the cloisters of the old monasteries. Early illustrations show the players patting a ball back and forth with the bare hand in the courtyard formed by the posts and pillars that held up the roof of the surrounding cloisters. The ball may well have been bounced off these in the early games because nets and rackets did not develop till later.

John Lydgate, a Benedictine monk and friend of Chaucer, wrote a poem in 1420 that said, 'Thus from post to pillar he was made to dance.' By the sixteenth century, people started saying from pillar to post when they meant someone was harassed from one place or predicament to another.

Up the spout

When something is ruined, lost, broken or destroyed, it is 'up the spout'.

Pawnbrokers used to put goods brought into their shops into a lift which carried them to a storeroom. The lift was known as 'the spout'. Only when the customer could afford to pay back his loan – plus interest – were the goods brought back 'down the spout'.

LAME DUCK

The Stock Exchange is well known for having bull and bear markets, but in earlier times it also had lame ducks, people who could not pay up on settlement day to cover the bargains they had struck.

David Garrick, one of England's greatest actors, coined the phrase in a play that he wrote in 1771: 'Change Alley bankrupts waddle out [like] lame ducks.'

During the convoys of World War II, torpedoed ships that were still afloat but unable to keep up with the other ships' speed were also called lame ducks. So are American office holders who fail or do not seek re-election but still have some months left in office until a new candidate takes over. Whether a person or an object, a lame duck is disabled or ineffectual.

To bandy words

Bandying words means to quarrel with somebody. The phrase comes from the Irish game of bandy which is similar to hockey, though much older. The players bandy the ball from side to side with a stick that is crooked at the end, and try to force it into the opponents' goal.

The saying, 'I'll not bandy words with you', has come across the sea from Ireland.

NAMBY-PAMBY

English poet Ambrose Philips wrote some sickly sentimental rhymes to flatter the daughters of influential friends. He called one child 'dimply damsel, sweetly smiling'. Another he described as 'timely blossom, infant fair'.

Some of his contemporaries in the eighteenth century took exception to the infantile odes and satirically twisted Ambrose's name into Namby-pamby, making it a byword for feeble childishness.

Philips, stung by being mocked, hung up a rod at the coffee house he frequented, threatening to use it on Alexander Pope, one of his main critics. But Pope kept his criticism verbal because Philips was also a skilled swordsman!

Red herring

This is a saying often used in politics. It means a person is trying to confuse an argument by talking about something slightly, or even totally, different from the main point in dispute.

The expression is a very old one and comes from fox hunting. It was believed that red herrings — or bloaters — would destroy the scent of a fox if they were dragged across the animal's trail. The pursuing dogs would then be confused and probably follow a false trail. In fact they would be chasing a 'red herring'.

WHEN MY SHIP COMES IN

Merchants who put up the money for the nineteenth-century trading ships to sail the seas to buy exotic cargoes from foreign lands were always waiting for their ship to come in.

If the ship returned safely from its hazardous journey, they would make a lot of money from the sale of the cargo. The phrase became synonymous with making a fortune.

The naked truth

If you tell the naked truth about somebody, it is the complete, absolute truth, including the bad points as well as the good ones.

The saying comes from an ancient fable in which Truth and Falsehood went for a swim in a lake. Falsehood got out first and put on Truth's clothes. But Truth could not bear the idea of dressing in Falsehood's garments, so he walked away naked.

THE NAKED TRUTH

WHAT A FIASCO

Although a fiasco now means any disastrous failure, the word started out as specifically applying to a theatre performance which flopped.

It comes from the Italian *far fiasco* – to make a flask – and meant to break down during a performance. Various incidents involving a flask in Italian theatrical history have been labelled as the origin, including a clown who blamed the flask he was using as a stage prop for failing to raise any laughs.

Kick the bucket

Meat is delivered to market today in huge refrigerated lorries, ready to be sold and distributed to all parts of the country. But in years gone by, the animals were taken to the market on foot and the whole process was far more chaotic, messy and literally bloody.

The cattle, pigs and sheep were slaughtered after reaching the market and their sometimes still kicking bodies hung on a wooden frame which was known as a bucket beam. This gruesome piece of equipment gave rise to the expression, 'He's kicked the bucket', when referring to a person who had died.

HALCYON DAYS

In Greek legend, Halcyone throws herself into the sea on learning in a dream that her husband, King Ceyx, has drowned in a storm. The gods are struck by her grief and transform the couple into kingfishers so that they can live happily as birds of the water.

As an extra boon, they and their descendants are promised that whenever they are hatching their eggs, on a nest of fishbones floating in the water, the seas will be untroubled by storms for fourteen days.

Although kingfishers nest on land beside streams, not floating at sea as the ancients thought, halcyon came to mean contentment and halcyon days a special period of calm, which the Greeks allocated to fourteen days during the winter solstice.

Welsh Rabbit

This cheap and tasty snack is, of course, melted cheese on toast. It became known some 300 years ago and to start with was something of a joke. At that time only the rich could afford to pay for the game from the royal preserves in Wales, so ordinary people rarely had the chance of tasting rabbit. With dry humour they began referring to melted cheese on toast – one of the few dishes they could afford – as their 'Welsh Rabbit'.

In later years snobbish people – or perhaps menu writers – tried to make the dish sound more fancy by calling it 'Welsh Rarebit'.

IN THE LIMELIGHT

Captain Thomas Drummond, a British army engineer in the 1820s, invented an intense white light produced by heating a piece of lime, in order to improve his map surveying capabilities in murky weather.

Drummond used his limelight for markers which could easily be observed in dull conditions when measuring distances by triangulation for map making. The scientific world welcomed his invention and started applying it to other uses, including lighthouses and theatrical lighting, where the leading actors found themselves in the full glare of bright light. Anyone in the limelight came to be in the focus of public interest.

Talking gibberish

When somebody talks quickly and in a way that is difficult to understand they are said to be talking gibberish, which is pretty insulting to the man who gave birth to the saying: an eleventh century Arabian alchemist called Geber who was in fact very intelligent.

Because his scientific knowledge and discoveries would have been considered blasphemous and therefore very dangerous for Geber, he developed an obscure jargon so that he could write his work without fear of discovery. His notes were meaningless to anybody else: Just 'Geberish'.

PIG IN THE MIDDLE

Pig in the middle was a rough-and-tumble children's game in which one child was encircled by others and had to escape them. In the gentler version, the pig in the middle has to intercept a ball thrown between the others.

Thus a person likened to the game is someone who is stuck unenviably between opposing groups of people.

A chip on his shoulder

Somebody who is by nature sulky, moody and argumentative, usually because he thinks others are against him, is said to have a chip on his shoulder.

Schoolboy rivals, particularly in America, gave birth to the saying nearly 200 years ago. It was the custom when two boys were spoiling for a fight for one to pick up a chip of wood and place it on his own shoulder. He would then challenge his opponent to knock it off. If the other boy did so, then they would begin to fight in earnest.

TALK TURKEY

Turkeys were originally wild fowl in North America and the story goes that a white settler went hunting with a Red Indian and tried to cheat him in dividing the spoil by keeping all the turkeys and giving the Indian all the buzzards.

By the 1820s, talking turkey meant speaking frankly or getting down to the hard facts, though Americans never developed the other side of the coin, talking buzzard, which presumably would have been to talk deceitfully.

Sour grapes

When you have desperately tried to get something but failed at the last moment, you will want to hide your disappointment. The most common way to do that is to pretend that you were not really all that interested in the first place. That's known as 'sour grapes'.

The saying comes from Aesop's ancient Greek fable about a fox drooling over bunches of grapes in a vineyard. After exhausting himself by leaping up, over and over again trying to reach them, he eventually gives up and slinks away. The fox tries to cover his frustration by saying: 'They're as sour as crabs, anyway!'

rigmarole

...is, then you do that, then you do another thing, then
...t a rigmarole'! That's just what we call a long,
...plicated way of doing things.

...ar-old expression began life as the Ragman Roll,
...dward I by Scottish noblemen. Each signed a deed
...y to the King and affixed his seal. The deeds were
...ether to form a document 40ft (12m) long!
...Roll is kept at the Public Records Office, London.

THE END

What a

First you do t
. . . oh, 'wha
involved, com
    The 700-ye
given to King
pledging loyal
then joined tog
The Ragman

The
'pitcl

R
stor
the
me

To go on strike

This has its roots in the eighteenth century when life at sea was lonely and cruel, with harsh punishments handed out to offenders. But seamen sometimes got together to fight their bad conditions. They would strike the sails of their ships – which means to lower them – so preventing the ship leaving port until their grievance was settled.

WIN ONE'S SPURS

When someone gains recognition in a sphere of achievement, he wins his spurs just as knights did in the medieval days of chivalry.

Under the codes of chivalry, a young nobleman began his training as a squire and wore silver spurs with which to urge on his horse. When he had shown sufficient valour to be dubbed a knight, he was ceremoniously tapped on the shoulder with a sword and also presented with a pair of gilt spurs to mark his elevation.

Several particularly fierce combats in the Middle Ages were called the Battle of the Spurs because of the huge number of gilt spurs found lying on the battlefield after the carnage.

Put a sock in it!

In these days of compact discs, videos and digital recordings, it is astonishing to think that only fifty years ago people used wind-up gramophones with the sound emerging from a large horn. A volume control was a thing of the future. So, when Aunt Agatha complained of that dreadful Charleston noise there was only one thing to do – put a sock in it – literally.

One or more woollen socks were pushed into the horn of the gramophone to muffle the sound. Today it means, quite simply; 'shut up'.

GO HAYWIRE

If someone goes haywire, they act in a crazy or disorganised way. The saying dates back to the early logging days in the forests of New England when the timber was hauled out by teams of horses or mules.

The animals were fed on bales of hay which were held together by wire. In a dilapidated or poorly equipped logging camp, the wire from the eaten bales would then be used to hold various bits of equipment together. The loggers would contemptuously call that type of camp a 'haywire outfit'.

Sent to Coventry

If you are sent to Coventry it means that people around you deliberately ignore you and will not speak to you because you have done something to upset them.

During the English Civil War there was such huge support in Coventry for the Parliamentarians that any Royalist prisoners from neighbouring Midland towns were sent there because it was certain they would receive no help. Indeed, the great majority of Coventry Parliamentarians not only refused to speak to the Royalists, but acted as though they didn't exist.

TOUCH AND GO

There you are, driving along, when suddenly another car pulls out and misses you by a fraction. It was a narrow escape, touch and go whether you would avoid an accident.

Sailors originally used 'touch and go' to describe any risky venture. Admiral William Smyth, who wrote the *Sailors' Word Book* in 1867, said it meant 'anything within an ace of ruin, as in rounding a ship very narrowly to escape rocks, or when, under sail, she rubs against the ground with her keel.'

The phrase could have started from the way the old sailing barges manoeuvred on the River Thames. They negotiated the channel by changing tack each time they touched bottom on the other side – very much touch and go, with the risk of getting stuck on the mud banks.

What a white elephant

A white elephant is a grand plan or scheme, usually fantastically expensive, but which, in real terms, is quite useless. Hundreds of years ago white elephants were regarded as sacred. To harm or neglect them was an offence punishable by death.

The King of Siam sometimes gave a white elephant to an enemy as a gift – knowing full well that he would probably be ruined, having to spend a fortune looking after it.

AUNT SALLY

Poor Aunt Sally, she is set up as the target of unreasonable attack.

She got her name in the nineteenth century at fairs and race meetings where the figure of a woman's head, with a pipe in its mouth, was set up as a variation of the game of skittles. The player had to break the pipe by throwing sticks at 'Aunt Sally'.

By the end of the century, Aunt Sally meant anyone who became the victim of unjustified criticism.

Barking up the wrong tree

If you complain or protest about something without good reason, or put the blame for something on the wrong person, you are barking up the wrong tree.

The saying comes from the practice of raccoon-hunting in America which has to be done at night when the small, furry animals are about. Dogs chase the raccoons and guide hunters to where they have seen them try to hide in branches. But sometimes, in the dark, the dogs make a mistake and 'bark up the wrong tree'.

PIN MONEY

A woman who wants to save or earn a little money for incidental expenses will call it her pin money.

In the sixteenth century when husbands had absolute control of the purse strings, wives started asking for a small sum to buy the handy new invention of pins so they could secure their hair, hat or shawl. From buying a few pins, women stretched their 'pin money' into a dress allowance or for buying other incidentals.

Cash on the nail

This saying means that you must pay cash immediately for your purchases. In this case, credit cards will not do nicely thank you.

It developed in the market places of England hundreds of years ago when a pole, or nail, was erected by traders.

They were the forerunners of shop counters – the buyer put his money on the nail and the seller put any change on the nail too, so everyone could see their dealing was done openly and fairly.

BOB'S YOUR UNCLE

All you have to do is one simple action and Bob's your uncle! You have attained something very easily.

Just like Arthur Balfour did in 1886. Lord Salisbury, the British Prime Minister, appointed Arthur to an important government post. Many considered the appointment was not made on merit but because 'Bob was his uncle'. He was the nephew of Lord Salisbury, whose Christian name was Robert, or Bob for short.

In fact Mr Balfour proved a formidable politician and later became Prime Minister himself.

Swinging the lead

A person who pretends to be working when he is doing nothing, or claims to be ill when there is nothing wrong with him, is said to be 'swinging the lead'.

Before today's sophisticated navigational equipment, seamen used to find out the depth of water by dropping a lead weight, attached to a thin, marked rope, to the bottom of a waterway.

Some lazy sailors, would take as long as possible about it. They would swing the lead to and fro several times instead of just dropping it straight into the water.

THE BITTER END

When you have finally completed an undertaking, no matter how difficult or unpleasant, you have seen it through to the bitter end.

This saying goes back four centuries to the days of sailing ships and had nothing to do with the sailors getting angry. Bitts were strong posts fastened on the deck of a ship for securing the anchor and other cables. When the rope was paid out to the bitter end, that was as far as it could go. Thus, when you have reached the bitter end, you cannot go any further.

Incidentally, a ship's posts for securing mooring lines and other cables are still called bitts today.

On your beam ends

When you are absolutely out of luck, out of money and out of much else besides, you are said to be 'on your beam ends'.

It's a phrase borrowed from old nautical times. A wooden ship depended for stability on its beams – the timbers that ran across the vessel, holding the sides in place and supporting the deck. A ship that was wrecked or so badly damaged that it was lying on its side, was 'on its beam ends'.

BUSMAN'S HOLIDAY

So, you're on a busman's holiday, spending your free time doing much the same thing as you do at work.

A few drivers of the old horse buses liked their animals so much that they spent their days off as passengers on their own buses, to check that the relief driver treated their teams all right. The horse bus reached its peak in London in 1901 when almost 4,000 of them were in service.

Working to a deadline

A deadline is the final time by which a job must be finished. Journalists use the word a lot. If they don't meet their deadline their work is useless – or 'dead' – because it will have missed the edition.

The phrase comes from the American Civil War in the 1860s. A line was marked all round the wire fence of the Andersonville prisoner-of-war camp and any prisoner seen crossing the line was, without warning, shot dead.

GONE FOR A BURTON

Something that is broken or lost is said to have gone for a Burton. The saying comes from a 1940s advertising campaign by an English brewery, Burton Ales in Staffordshire.

Their posters showed well-known groups of people with one obvious person missing and the words: 'He's gone for a Burton'. With typical dry humour, World War II pilots in Britain adopted the phrase for the fate of airmen who failed to return.

Apple of your eye

If someone referred to you as the apple of their eye it would mean that they are particularly fond of you – usually when you've done something to make them proud!

It was long believed that the pupil of the eye was a round, solid ball – rather like an apple. For that reason the pupil was called the eye's apple.

Sight, of course, has always been held as one of man's most precious assets. So anybody deeply cherished by another person became as important to him as 'the apple of his eye'.

PEEPING TOM

Society hates a Peeping Tom, a voyeur who furtively pries on scenes that are none of his business. The original Peeping Tom was a tailor when Lady Godiva made her famous ride naked through the English town of Coventry in the eleventh century.

Lady Godiva was the wife of Leofric, Earl of Mercia, whose domain included Coventry. Exasperated by her pleas to reduce the town's taxes, he agreed to do so only if she rode naked through the market place. She dumbfounded him by doing so. By way of thanks, the townspeople saved her blushes by staying indoors and closing their shutters.

All, that is, except Tom the Tailor. To his disgrace, he peeped. The story goes that he was struck blind for his wickedness.

Caught eavesdropping

There are a lot of stories in the news today about 'phone-tapping' and 'bugging'. People who do it are the high-technology counterparts of the centuries-old 'eavesdropper' – somebody who listens in to other people's private conversations.

The eaves of a house are the parts of the roof that stick out over the walls, protecting them from falling water. The space on the ground where the water falls was known originally as the 'eavesdrip' and later as the 'eavesdrop'. This was the area where people like blackmailers, or even detectives, would hide, hoping to hear what was going on in the house. Such people became known as 'eavesdroppers'.

RUNNING THE GAUNTLET

An unpopular politician could soon tell you what running the gauntlet means today: to be attacked on all sides.

He would expect only a verbal onslaught but running the gauntlet used to be physical punishment, first used in Sweden where *lopp* meant running and *gata* meant lane, anglicised into gauntlet.

The British Navy adopted the punishment in 1661. Theft was abhorred aboard ship and the culprit was made to run between two lines of sailors each armed with a rope. The Royal Navy abolished the practice in 1813 but it lingered on in public schools where offenders had to run between rows of boys striking out with fists or wet towels.

To put a spoke in your wheel

If you are trying to get on with something and somebody does something to stop you, they have 'put a spoke in your wheel'.

In olden days the wheels on carts were solid, but they had one or two holes in which the driver could place a pin. This pin, or spoke as it was called, was used either in the same way as a parking brake on the modern car, or to prevent the cart running out of control, as a horse could not go far if it had to drag the spoked wheels.

THE ACID TEST

In the eighteenth and nineteenth centuries, a crude but certain way of testing whether gold was real or fake was to see if it withstood the highly corrosive effect of aquafortis, as nitric acid was then called.

Nitric acid dissolves most metals but gold is an exception. So if a sample withstood aquafortis, it had passed the original acid test. Being colourless, it bore the Latin name for strong water. Today's methods for testing gold are far more refined, but the acid test survives to mean any crucial test.

A flash in the pan

A 'flash in the pan' describes somebody who shows great promise, then fails to live up to expectations.

For example, a darts player might score the maximum 180 with his first three darts. Onlookers think he is a potential champion. But he is unable to repeat it. His earlier success was a mere 'flash in the pan'.

The expression came from the early seventeenth-century flintlock — a very unreliable musket. When its owner pulled the trigger there would often be a dramatic flash in the lock-pan. But the powder failed to ignite so the gun would not fire.

RAINING CATS AND DOGS

It may seem odd to associate cats and dogs with a downpour of rain and raging winds. But there's good reason.

First the cats: They were the devil's animal in folk belief and were thought to have power over good and evil. That power extended to control over the weather. The superstitious believed that if a cat washed its face, that meant rain. If seen leaping or clawing, that was an omen of gales.

Now the dogs: Odin was a Viking god and his attendant was a dog, which symbolized the wind.

When we have torrential rain, it's therefore raining cats and dogs.

Tell it to the Marines

People who relate stories that nobody believes are often told 'go tell it to the Marines!'

Just over 300 years ago Charles II didn't believe a word when a traveller told him he had seen flying fish. But when a Marine vouched for the story, the King decreed it must be true. He said, 'No class of our subjects can have so wide a knowledge of seas and lands as the men of our loyal Maritime Regiment of Foot'.

Henceforward, ere ever we cast doubts about a tale that lacks likelihood, we will first 'tell it to the Marines'.

A LOAD OF BUNKUM

It had to be a politician who invented this saying! His name was Felix Walker, an American congressman who represented Buncombe County in North Carolina.

He surpassed himself for talking rubbish during a debate in the House of Representatives in the 1820s. When taken to task for time wasting, he said, 'I was not speaking to the House, but to Buncombe.' This evolved into talking a load of bunkum or bunk whenever anyone speaks a lot of nonsense.

Sold down the river

If somebody betrays you or breaks a promise, then they are said to have 'sold you down the river'.

The phrase arose in the United States in the last century when rich American householders would sell their slaves to plantation owners. The slaves would have to leave the relative comforts of the big houses and be transported down the Mississippi river to a harsh and cruel life on the plantation.

POSH PEOPLE

They are the people who live in style, doing the right things and going to the right places. And it was part of that lifestyle which created the term posh.

In the days of the British Empire, experienced travellers going by steamship to India booked their cabins port side out, starboard home – POSH for short – so that in each direction they would be on the cooler side of the ship, sheltered from the sun.

Chancing your arm

Somebody who takes a risk to gain an advantage for himself is 'chancing his arm'.

It was originally a military saying and referred to the fact that insignia of rank, like badges or stripes, were worn on the arm of a soldier's uniform. If he broke the King's Regulations in any way, he was 'chancing (that is, risking) his arm'.

THE COLD SHOULDER

You know when you are being given the cold shoulder. You are ignored, frozen out, made to feel unwelcome.

In days of old, the cold shoulder was literally given to guests who had outstayed their welcome. If the host felt the guest had lingered for too many days of wining and dining, along came the big hint. The cold leftovers of lamb, normally fit only for servants, would be served on a plate. Exit guest.

Feeling badgered

If you tease or annoy somebody and will not leave them alone, you are said to be badgering them.

The saying comes from the cruel medieval sport of badger-baiting. The poor animal was put into a large, upturned barrel, then dogs were sent in to drag him out. When they emerged, the badger was separated from the tormenting hounds and sent back in the barrel to recover – only for the dogs to be unleashed upon him over and over again.

ACHILLES' HEEL

An Achilles' heel is a small but fatal weakness, the one that killed the legendary hero of Greek mythology.

Achilles was the son of the sea goddess Thetis, who dipped him into the River Styx as a child to make him invincible. The one part she forgot to dip was his heel because she was holding him by the ankle.

As a warrior in the Trojan Wars, Achilles' body was invulnerable until he was fatally wounded by an arrow in the heel which struck his one weak point.

A baker's dozen . . .

This phrase means, quite simply, thirteen, not twelve. It comes from olden days when bread was the staple diet of the population and there were heavy penalties for any baker whose loaves were of short weight.

So to make sure they didn't fall foul of the law, many bakers used to add an extra loaf — called the vantage loaf — to each batch of twelve.

BORN WITH A SILVER SPOON IN HIS MOUTH

If people think someone has always been very rich, they will say he was born with a silver spoon in his mouth.

The saying goes back to the sixteenth and seventeenth centuries when it was customary for godchildren of wealthy families to be given sets of silver spoons as christening presents. Silver remains a traditional christening present among those who can afford it, though the baby of rich parents is far less likely to be fed with a silver spoon these days.

Not enough room to swing a cat

When an estate agent describes a house as 'compact' what he probably really means is that it is tiny — that there is 'not enough room to swing a cat'.

The 'cat' in this centuries-old saying is not a furry puss but the dreaded nine-thonged whip, known as the 'cat o' nine tails' that was used to punish sailors. The punishment always took place on deck because below there was 'not enough room to swing a cat'.

THAT'S CLAPTRAP

Quiz show presenters are the masters of claptrap these days. When they introduce a contestant and pause for the audience to clap after naming his home town or occupation, they have set a trap to win applause. That's claptrap.

The phrase came from the theatre in the eighteenth century when actors set up showy, sentimental expressions particularly designed to win applause. They even developed mechanical clappers to add to the atmosphere. But the expressions came to be recognised as rubbish. That is what claptrap means today, a lot of nonsense.

Conspiracy of silence

If you are the victim of a 'conspiracy of silence' you are convinced –
often wrongly – that your friends or associates are trying to keep a
secret from you.

The expression was first used in Victorian times by a poet named
Sir Lewis Morris. In truth he was not very good, but he wanted to
become Poet Laureate. He complained to writer Oscar Wilde, that
people were jealous of him and so refused to discuss his poetry.
'There is a conspiracy of silence against me. What shall I do?' he
asked. Oscar replied 'Join it'.

BY HOOK OR BY CROOK

Hook and crook were medieval reaping tools, the curved billhook with its sharp edge for cutting and the crook for holding the corn while it was cut.

The story goes that King William Rufus of England was slain by an arrow in the back on a hunting expedition in the New Forest in 1100. His brother, Henry, rode off to claim the throne. Sir Walter Tyrrel, who fired the arrow, fled to France, and the others in the hunting party dispersed, leaving the body lying on the ground. A charcoal burner named Purkiss was the one who found the body of the disliked tyrant and took it for burial. As his reward, he won the right to gather firewood that he could reach with his hook and crook.

It was hardly the easiest way to collect wood but guaranteed that the trees would be pruned instead of felled, and peasants were not normally allowed to cut firewood in the king's hunting forest. By hook or by crook now means to achieve something by all means fair or foul.

Bless you!

When somebody sneezes people often call out 'Bless you!' It is a custom which is thought to date back to the great plague in the seventeenth century when at least 80,000 people died in London alone.

A sneeze was believed to be the first sign of the horrific disease. But it's also said that in medieval times people believed that when a person sneezed his soul momentarily left his body.

So that the Devil could not capture the temporarily unguarded soul, by-standers quickly called 'God bless you!' The protected soul would then return to the safety of the body and the Devil would be thwarted.

CURATE'S EGG

A curate's egg is a mixed blessing, good in parts, bad in others.

The description is almost a hundred years old and comes from a cartoon that set a lot of clergymen laughing in sympathy when published in 1895 in the weekly *Punch* magazine in London. The assistant to an Anglican bishop used to be called a curate and he was obviously not in a position to cross his senior. In the cartoon, an unfortunate curate is dining with his bishop, who says, 'I'm afraid you've got a bad egg, Mr Jones.' The curate tactfully replies, 'Oh no, my lord, I assure you parts of it are excellent.'

Waging a Battle Royal . . .

A keenly-fought contest between two people or two teams is said to be a 'Battle Royal'. It can refer to any game, from a chess tournament to a rugby match.

But it was no harmless pastime that gave birth to the saying – it was the horrific, now outlawed, 'sport' of cockfighting. Sixteen birds were pitted (put into a pit) against each other. The eight winners in the first 'round' were then matched and so on until just two cocks were left. The survivor was the 'king' – champion of the Battle Royal.

PLEASED AS PUNCH

Someone pleased as Punch could not be more proud of themselves, just like the puppet in the popular old show.

An Italian actor began the character under the name of Pulcinella or Punchinello in the seventeenth century and it was taken up by puppeteers all over Europe. They played 'Punch and Judy' shows at fairs and entertainment booths at the seaside and still do so occasionally today as children's entertainment.

The glove puppet of Punch usually appears as grotesque and hump-backed with a large red nose. Yet he is very pleased with himself as he clowns around, performing dreadful deeds like beating his wife Judy and dropping the baby. Anything particularly outrageous is accompanied by his insincere comment, 'What a pity!'

Face the music

If you are caught doing something wrong then (gulp!) you will just
have to summon up all your courage and accept whatever
punishment is coming. You will, in fact 'face the music'.

One theory says the saying comes from the plight of a nervous
actor or entertainer who, when the curtain goes up, must literally
face the music, as the orchestra is in the 'pit' in front of him.

Others think the expression dates back to the time when soldiers
who were dismissed from the army for dishonourable conduct
were drummed out of the service. They were literally 'facing the
music'.

LEFT IN THE LURCH

A person abandoned in a position of great difficulty is left in the lurch. The saying goes all the way back to the sixteenth century when 'lurch' meant a swindle.

So its origin could have come from the victim of the swindle, abandoned by those who had hoodwinked him and left in the lurch.

At the same time, lurch was the word used to denote a particular score at the end of various card games such as whist, when the winner was well ahead of the others. The losers were certainly left in a difficult situation because the winner had 'lurched' or left them far behind.

Bonfire night

We all know that bonfire night is held as a celebration on November 5 to mark the failure of Guy Fawkes and his fellow plotters to blow up the Houses of Parliament in 1605.

Bonfires go back a lot further than that. In the fifteenth century it had become a custom on a certain day to light three fires in honour of St John. Little is now known about the ceremony. But we do know that the first fire was made entirely of animal bones and was called a bone fire. The second, made only of wood, was a wood fire, and the third, wood and bones, was called St John's fire.

Our word bonfire comes of course, from the original, gruesome bone fire.

COCK A SNOOK

When you cock a snook at someone, you are showing contempt for them.

Snooks was an old word for the derisive gesture of placing a thumb on the nose. English street urchins of the nineteenth century would complete their show of derision for authority by cocking, or lifting, their nose upwards. Their other saucy trick was to put their tongue in their cheek.

Eventually the phrase meant showing contempt whether or not the gesture was actually performed.

What a load of old codswallop!

When somebody says something which is nonsense, far-fetched, or simply untrue, they are often accused of speaking 'a load of old codswallop'.

We have a certain American gent called Hiram Codd to thank for this colourful expression. In 1875 he patented a special bottle of mineral water which became very popular – except among hardened beer drinkers.

The word 'wallop' was already well in use to describe alcoholic drinks and so, sneeringly, Hiram's concoction – and other weak drinks – became known in bars as 'Codd's Wallop'. Gradually, anything inferior or false became known by the single word 'codswallop'.

143

HAM ACTOR

A ham actor is a truly dreadful one whose performance is so shallow or over-played that the audience deride him. The term arose within the theatrical profession when the full slang word for incompetence on stage was 'hamfatter'.

Theatre flourished as popular entertainment in nineteenth century America but money was often short and the cheapest way to remove greasepaint make-up was by using the fat from ham. The verdict of contempt for a fellow actor therefore was to call him a hamfatter.

The life of Reilly

Anybody living the 'life of Reilly' (sometimes spelt 'Riley') is surrounded by luxury and has no cares or worries.

The saying has emerged from the music hall days of the Victorian era. One popular song of the time was about an Irishman – actually named O'Reilly – who dreamed of the luxury life ahead once he made his fortune. The song was called 'Are you the O'Reilly?' and the chorus, which the audience sang, went: 'Are you the O'Reilly who keeps this hotel? Are you the O'Reilly they speak of so well? Are you the O'Reilly they speak of so highly? Cor blimey, O'Reilly, you are looking well'.

COLD ENOUGH TO FREEZE THE BALLS OFF A BRASS MONKEY

This is not as rude as it sounds. A brass or iron monkey was a type of cannon in the seventeenth century.

The cannon balls were stacked in pyramids but if it was cold enough, the pyramids tumbled over because the iron balls contracted more quickly than the brass trays in which they were stacked.

So if it's cold enough to freeze the balls off a brass monkey, the weather is extreme.

The unkindest cut of all

These days we often hear of 'cuts' and when something cherished has to go – perhaps a hospital wing or a sports complex – the local newspaper might well refer to it as 'the unkindest cut of all'.

But the saying is no invention of a headline writer. It comes from Act III, scene two of Shakespeare's play, *Julius Caesar*. After the assassination of the emperor, Mark Anthony tells the Romans: 'This was the most unkindest cut of all.'

Shakespeare is the source of many popular sayings today. 'Mum's the Word' for example, comes from Henry IV, Part two; 'Seal your lips and give no words but – mum.'

MIND YOUR PS AND QS

People who mind their Ps and Qs are careful about their behaviour, a far cry from the unruly waterfront bars where sailors used to drink.

Some inn keepers would give them credit until payday, chalking up on a slate how many pints and quarts they had ordered, abbreviated to P and Q. They had to mind their Ps and Qs to keep the record straight.

By the nineteenth century, children were admonished to mind their Ps and Qs but teachers did not mention the lowly origins. The more genteel explanation was that the letter p was easy to muddle with q.

That takes the cake

Originally this saying was used when somebody's efforts in a contest were so good that they were bound to carry off first prize. Later the expression was used mockingly of people who had said something silly or outrageous.

In the deep south of the United States in the last century negroes held competitions to see who could walk in the most graceful or imaginative way around a cake on the floor. The winner would literally 'take the cake'.

TILT AT WINDMILLS

In that classic of western literature, the self-appointed knight errant Don Quixote mistakes an array of windmills for giants whom he must slay.

He charges the first windmill but his lance gets entangled and he is spun round by the sail until he falls back to earth. Miguel de Cervantes intended the adventures of his elderly knight to be a satire on chivalry, prevalent when he wrote the book in 1605.

The allusion to windmills has stayed with us as meaning to attack imaginary or impractical foes.

Soap opera

Anybody who has never heard of J. R., Alexis Carrington or Bet Lynch and Pauline Fowler must have been living on a different planet lately. They are, of course, all characters from TV soap operas which attract millions of viewers every week.

The idea of serialised melodrama with a cliff-hanging finish to each episode is nothing new. They began in the United States when there were few television sets around and radio was at its popularity peak. At that time half a dozen or more serials were on the air each week. The link? They were nearly all sponsored by soap-makers. And so the phrase 'soap opera' was born.

HOLD THE FORT

During the American civil war, Union General John Murray Corse was attacked by the Confederates at Allatoona Pass in 1864. General William Sherman sent him a signal saying, 'Hold the fort. I am coming.'

Corse gallantly fought on, and Sherman's phrase passed into language, popularised in a hymn and in literature. It now means to keep things going or take temporary charge.

The Jeep

The Jeep is, of course, the amazing four-wheel drive vehicle which is now popular all over the world.

It is so called because after it was designed in the US during the second world war it was listed by the army as a GP (general purpose) vehicle. The initials GP rapidly became the word 'Jeep'.

The army is also responsible for another well-used word in the motoring world, DERV — for use in a Diesel Engine Road Vehicle. You can now buy 'derv' from almost any garage.

PARTING SHOT

The horsemen of Parthia had a real battle to keep the Roman Empire from encroaching on their ancient kingdom in western Asia, now part of Iran. They had a particular trick of firing their arrows backwards while pretending to be in flight.

This manoeuvre, the Parthian shot, staved off the Romans. Anglicised as 'the parting shot', it is now taken as having the final and most effective word in a debate.

Between the devil and the deep blue sea

Somebody who is in a very difficult situation and is liable to be in real trouble whichever course of action he chooses is said to be 'between the devil the deep blue sea'. The devil in this case is not 'Old Nick', but the heavy wooden beam which used to be fixed to the sides of ships as a support for the big guns. It was called the gunwhale and was a very difficult place to get to, calling for great agility on the part of the luckless sailor ordered to that position.

One slip and . . . splash! He was literally between the devil and the deep blue sea.

PLAY POSSUM

The furry little opossum feigns death when it is threatened or attacked. No other creature plays death quite so well, lying limply on its side with its tongue hanging out and eyes shut.

Slave owners in America's deep south who suspected slaves of shamming sickness to avoid work would claim he was 'coming possum over us'. The slave trade came to an end, but playing possum survived as meaning to pretend illness or death.

Staging a boycott

In the 1850s, a very strict and unbending retired English army officer, Captain Charles Cunningham Boycott, was a land agent on an estate in County Mayo, Ireland.

Because of several bad harvests, the tenants were very poor. But Boycott refused to reduce rents and ordered anybody in arrears to be evicted. His servants walked out and people refused to work for him.

In the end, he fled back to England – victim of the world's first 'boycott'.

PIE IN THE SKY

Joe Hill, an early American union leader, wrote a song which warned workers not to be exploited by their employers. 'You'll get pie in the sky when you die,' he said.

At that time, pie was associated with wealth because it was a slang word for treat, like the rewards drawn from bran pie, the old name for dipping for hidden prizes in the bran tub. His song turned the phrase into meaning false promises, utopian dreams that are never realized.

Hill belonged to a labour organisation, the Industrial Workers of the World, which was very radical. He was executed in 1915 on a murder charge which his associates said was trumped up in order to get rid of the unrest he caused. Just before his death, he said, 'Don't waste any time in mourning. Organise.'

To get the sack

A person who has been dismissed from his job is often said to have 'got the sack'. Years ago this would have been true – literally. Because workmen used to own their own tools of trade and carry them round in a sack.

   When they got a job the employer would look after their tools, but when the worker was no longer needed or wanted he would be given back his sack and told to look for work elsewhere.

GRASS WIDOW

The wives of officers serving in India during the days of British colonial rule stayed up in the cool of the hill stations while their husbands served through the worst heat on the hot dusty plains.

They were called grass widows, not because the grass grew on the cooler heights but from the idea of being sent away on holiday or turned out to grass, as horses were sent to pasture after work. Thus, by the mid-1850s, a grass widow signified a married woman whose husband was temporarily absent.

Wet behind the ears

Somebody who is not very experienced in life can make comments or express opinions that more mature people dismiss with a smile. They think the person has not shown a full understanding of the subject and say, 'Oh, he's still wet behind the ears'.

The expression is very old and refers to the fact that many animals, when they are born, have a small depression behind each ear. Of course, the creature is wet when new-born, and the last place to dry is the little area behind each ear. When that is dry, the animal is a little older and perhaps a little wiser.

CRY WOLF

In all the different versions of a very old fable, the shepherd boy keeps playing a trick on his neighbours by shouting, 'Wolf'. But he cried wolf so often that when a real wolf came and attacked his flock, nobody believed him and the sheep were killed. Crying wolf is raising a false alarm.

A bear garden

If a father came into his sons' bedroom and found a pillow-fight in progress, he might shout: 'It's like a bear garden in here'. In effect, it is a place of turmoil and confusion.

In King Henry VIII's time, bear-baiting was very popular. So much so that gardens were set aside for the 'sport'. These 'bear gardens' were well known for scenes of utter chaos, shouting and fighting.

SAVE FACE

The English community living in China in the nineteenth century were struck by the elaborate methods employed by the Chinese to avoid giving or receiving humiliation.

The English somewhat mistakenly called this saving face, though what the Chinese were worried about was *tiu lien*, which means losing face. Nonetheless, saving face means avoiding disgrace or embarrassment.

The hair of the dog

After a party, it is not unusual for some of the guests to wake up the next morning with a hangover. The cure is said to be another drink, or 'the hair of the dog'.

This is based on the superstition that people who are ill after being bitten by a dog can only be cured by swallowing a piece of burnt hair from the same animal. In truth, the 'cure' seldom works.

IN A PRETTY PICKLE

This saying comes from the Dutch words *in de pekel zitten*, sitting in the pickle, which was literally the brine or vinegar in which food was placed to preserve it.

When people began using the phrase in the sixteenth century to indicate a sorry plight, they said ill pickle. But these days we say pretty pickle or fine pickle to add emphasis to the mess.

America's Cup

This world-famous ocean-going yacht race got its name because
of a bit of cheek on the part of the Americans.

The race began more than a hundred years ago and the idea was
that the winning crew would be presented with a trophy – the
Hundred-Guinea Cup – by the Royal Yacht Squadron.

Then the unthinkable happened. The United States entered a
schooner, appropriately called *America* and won! The Yankee
victors were so pleased with themselves that they promptly
renamed the trophy America's Cup – and it's been that way ever
since.

SPITTING IMAGE

The spitting image is an exact likeness and came from seventeenth-century folk who would say of their father, for example, that we are 'as like him as if spit out of his mouth'.

The old form was spittan or spitten, even the spit and image. Now it's easier to say as 'spitting image'.

Let the devil take the hindmost

Somebody who doesn't care too much about the result of his actions might well say: 'Let the devil take the hindmost'. It means that he is willing to take the risk and gamble that the result will be a success, for himself at least.

The saying is based on a medieval belief that the devil ran a training school for his followers. There was a leaving ceremony in which the 'students' had to run through a special underground passageway. The last person was 'the hindmost'. He was captured by the devil and had to stay as a slave.

169

SHOW A LEG

Some ships in the British navy used to allow women aboard. A few wives were even aboard in battle, carrying gunpowder and bandaging the wounded. They had the privilege of getting an extra half-hour lying-in after the men got up to do the ship-board jobs.

In the morning, the officer would call out, 'Show a leg'. All those with hairy legs in the hammocks had to get up. The curvaceous female ones could stay where they were. It's not quite like that today, but show a leg still means get a move on.

To come up to scratch

A person who passes a test or in some other way meets a required standard is said to have 'come up to scratch'.

The saying comes from the sport of prize-fighting, popular throughout Britain in the last century. There were no set rounds of three minutes, as is the case in boxing today. Instead the round went on until one of the fighters was knocked down.

Then, after a pause of 30 seconds, a count of eight began. If the fighter failed in that time to reach a mark scratched in the centre of the ring, he was beaten. He had failed 'to come up to scratch'.

BEE IN THE BONNET

In olden times, a muddled person was described as having bees in the brain because of the straightforward analogy to having too many ideas buzzing around the head.

English poet Robert Herrick took the idea forward with a popular poem in 1648 called *The Mad Maid's Song*. The obsessed maiden cries, 'For pity, Sir, find out that bee, which bore my love away. I'll seek him in your bonnet brave, I'll seek him in your eyes.' A bee in the bonnet then entered currency as being obsessed with an idea.

Ship-shape and Bristol fashion

In the fifteenth century, Bristol was one of England's most important ports. Its biggest claim to sea-faring fame is that John Cabot and his three sons set off from Bristol in the reign of Henry VII to discover Newfoundland.

Survival on such perilous journeys in those days meant that the ships and equipment had to be in perfect working order. The men spent many hours making sure this was so. Anything that was well prepared, neat, tidy and efficient therefore came to be known as all 'ship-shape and Bristol fashion'.

DOG IN THE MANGER

In one of Aesop's fables, a dog stations itself in a manger and stops the oxen and horses from eating the hay although it has no use for the fodder itself.

Thus, a churlish person who grudges others using something he does not want for himself is described as 'dog in the manger'.

His name is mud

John Wilkes Booth, the man who assassinated American President Abraham Lincoln in 1865, broke a leg while making his getaway. He called at the home of Doctor Samuel Mudd who treated his injury. The following day Dr Mudd was arrested and charged with conspiring to murder the President. He was sentenced to life imprisonment.

It was later established that Dr Mudd knew nothing of Booth's crime. He was pardoned and freed. But that could not prevent his name giving birth to the expression; 'His name is mud', referring to anybody who is thought of as disreputable or who is held in contempt.

HOODLUM

A reporter in nineteenth-century San Francisco wanted to write about a gang of street criminals led by a man called Muldoon. To escape reprisal, he spelled the name backwards as Noodlum, but a printer on the paper used an 'H' by mistake and produced Hoodlum.

This is the favourite story for the origin of the slang word for gangster. Some sticklers claim that they cannot find the story about Noodlum or Hoodlum in the old newspaper files, but let them come up with a better one!

Robbing Peter to pay Paul

People in financial difficulties sometimes try to juggle their money around in an attempt to solve their problems. They might pay one bill with money that should really have been used to pay somebody else. This is called 'robbing Peter to pay Paul'.

The expression goes back to the sixteenth century when urgent repairs were needed to St Paul's Cathedral but little cash was available for the purpose. To solve the problem the Abbey Church of St Peter, Westminster, which had been created a cathedral only ten years earlier in 1550, was 'demoted' back to an abbey church. Many of its estates – and the income from them – were appropriated to St Paul's. Thus, St Peter was 'robbed' to pay St Paul.

GO THROUGH THE HOOP

One of the most famous circus tricks, still popular after two centuries, is to jump through a hoop of blazing fire on horseback. The bareback rider can also vault from the horse, bursting through a paper hoop to land again on its back.

Fewer people go to the circus now to witness these feats, but going through the hoop became the equivalent of undergoing a trial or ordeal.

Ringing the changes

If you are stuck in an uneventful job, or have to do the same task over and over again, you are likely out of sheer boredom to try to find different ways of going about it. That's known as 'ringing the changes'.

The saying comes, not surprisingly, from the art of bell-ringing. A set of three bells tuned to the diatonic scale can be rung in a series of six variations.

But somewhere with a set of twelve bells, such as Canterbury Cathedral, offers nearly 500 million variations. Somebody once calculated it would take thirty-eight years to ring all the changes at Canterbury!

NOT WORTH THE RUSH

This saying comes from such early medieval times that no one knows for certain if it refers to the tallowed rush used for lighting or to the fresh green rushes which were strewn on the floor for important visitors as the original welcome mat.

Whether rush light or rush floor, the visitor not worth a rush was of no importance. Since the custom of using rushes is long forgotten, we equally use the phrase these days for articles of no value where once it only applied to people.

The V-sign

One of the most common gestures of anger today, often between car drivers, is the V-sign; two fingers raised upwards to the person who has annoyed you.

Its origins are uncertain, but one strong theory is that it began during the Hundred Years' War between England and France in the fourteenth and fifteenth centuries. Captured English archers had the two first fingers of their right hand cut off so that they couldn't take part in future battles.

It then became the custom of the English, after felling a Frenchman with an arrow, defiantly to raise his two fingers aloft to show he was still very much involved in the fight and as if to say; 'there's more where that came from!'

181

THE MOMENT OF TRUTH

The moment of truth comes directly from the Spanish *el momento de la verdad*, the point in the bull fight when the matador makes the final sword thrust.

Ernest Hemingway wrote about it in his widely read novel *Death in the Afternoon* in 1932, making outsiders aware that the Spanish described this end to the bull fight as the moment of truth. It came to mean any turning point or time of revelation.

In the nick of time

Something that happens 'in the nick of time' is a last moment reprieve from failure, like a goal at the end of extra time in a soccer match. And when the giant computerised scoreboard at a stadium like Wembley flashes up the message, 'Wow, what a goal!' it is only a modern version of a man with a stick of wood.

For hundreds of years the scores in games similar to soccer were kept by a man who would 'nick' the side of a tally stick each time a team scored. If victory came for one of the sides at the last moment, it was known as the 'nick in time'.

CURRY FAVOUR

This has nothing to do with eating curry and originally had very little to do with favour because the original fifteenth-century saying was to curry favel.

In those days the only currying that went on was to curry, or groom, a horse. The act of stroking the horse down came to be associated with flattery or blandishments. Favel was the name of a chestnut horse, presumably a showy one that was not as reliable or good as he appeared, because currying favel meant using insincere flattery. Favel has passed out of equine history and instead we regard humans who curry favour as ingratiating themselves.

Index